Gail Muller

Do Hope

Why you should never give up.

**Dedicated to my nieces, Darcy and Agnes,
who have made my life better in every way.**

Published by
The Do Book Company 2023
Works in Progress Publishing Ltd
thedobook.co

Text © Gail Muller 2023
Photography © Jim Marsden 2023

10 9 8 7 6 5 4 3 2 1

To find out more about our company,
books and authors, please visit
thedobook.co or follow us **@dobookco**

5 per cent of our proceeds from the sale
of this book is given to The DO Lectures
to help it achieve its aim of making
positive change: thedolectures.com

Cover designed by James Victore
Book designed and set by Ratiotype

Printed and bound by OZGraf Print on
Pergraphica, an FSC® certified paper

A CIP catalogue record for this book is
available from the British Library

ISBN 978-1-914168-24-6

Contents

Prologue   7

Introduction   10

Part 1: Hope and the Three Musketeers

1   Why I have hope   19

2   Musketeer one: Resilience   31

3   Musketeer two: Perseverance   41

4   Musketeer three: Self-worth   49

Part 2: Be captain of your own team

5   Who is cheering for you?   59

6   Failure is a gift   73

7   Adversity is your ally   81

Part 3: How to use hope to fuel your tank

8   Find the gold under your feet   91

9   Tools   95

10   A little bit of hope goes a long way   107

Resources   121

About the author   123

Thanks   124

Prologue

The moment I was told to let go of hope was the same moment I defiantly lashed myself to it, as if to the mast of a raft in a storm. In defiance of defeat, I was keeping myself tied fast to hope when those I looked to for it had no lifebelt to throw me. Hope, back then, was all I had. Turns out that it was exactly what I needed. Perhaps it's what you need too ...

It had taken years to get to this room, the room where I thought I might finally get an answer, or at least some insights, into my many years of chronic illness. I was 32 years old and in the pain clinic of my local hospital, feeling like I'd arrived at the last chance saloon for relief and respite.

I sat, uncomfortably, facing one of the top specialist doctors in the department, and willed him to speak a solution into life. I'd worked so hard to keep myself going, always believing that there would be an answer if I just looked hard enough and kept trying, and now I was here with someone who was on my side, someone knowledgeable about pain who would surely help lift me out of my exhausted agony.

After asking me how I had been doing and listening to my earnest tales of all the new things I'd been trying, he held my gaze as my eyes pleaded with him to tell me the next steps I could take. Instead, in that quiet, tired and impersonal room, he told me to let go of hope.

'Hope is holding you back,' he said. And as I stared at him in crushed disbelief, he explained that it would be better to accept my condition and adapt to it, rather than keep on searching for a way to get 'better'. He posited that 'better' wasn't an option. Only acceptance was. And hope, he said, had no place in that equation.

The pain clinic back then was different to now, and I think with hindsight I understand the message he was trying to give me. But on that day, it was the final lifebuoy being pulled away from me. On that particular day, my outlook on life changed. I realised that outsourcing some things to qualified specialists was all well and good, but I wasn't going to be told how to manage my desire to thrive, heal or hope for better. Those were reasons to stay alive, to keep moving forward and to find a pathway through adversity, and they were mine alone to decide how to use.

I made it clear that I didn't agree with him, and I left the hospital. I wasn't angry or rebelling. I wasn't raging against sensible things like the medication that gave me my ability to function, but I *was* railing against the idea of giving up. I sailed out of the hospital that day lashed tightly to my mast of Hope into the stormy waters of what was to come. Towards an incredible future I didn't know was possible, but that I hoped could be.

Introduction

Forget your perfect offering
There is a crack, a crack in everything
That's how the light gets in.

Anthem, Leonard Cohen

Hope.

We have all invoked it, tried to feel it, or willed it to take us forward. But what does the word 'hope' really mean, and how can we feel more of it?

Why do we collectively seem to need hope more than ever?

The concept of hope can be seen as esoteric, its meaning chameleon-like. It is often seen as a *wish*, perhaps whimsical or fantastical, but hope is *not* this. It is more closely aligned with a sense of optimism, and a pragmatic vision of one or multiple pathways to a place or state that you intend to reach.

Hope is, by proxy, a testament to not giving up. A railing against failing. It's what we lean on when we have nothing concrete to give. No firm, empirical assurances. Just a desire and vision of something better. A vote for a brighter day, a better future, and the patience, energy and resilience to get us there.

Hope acts as the energy charge that propels us from misery into forward momentum.

Life isn't easy, but it can get better

Are you facing some challenges? Feeling a bit overwhelmed? Try not to worry, you're not alone.

Things are going to improve just like you hope they will.

You're not perfect, and that's okay. In fact, it's more than okay, it's exactly how you're meant to be. As Cohen so wisely said, everything has a crack in it so that the light can reach you. The things you might consider difficult or broken about yourself, or the world around you, are actually the chinks where the sun can pour in to help you grow. To shine the light into your inner world, showing you where you need to focus your energy.

You're not supposed to get things right all the time, and you're absolutely *not* meant to get through this life blemish-free, unscathed and having never screwed up. In fact, the very things about you that have been broken and show flaws are the parts that can end up being the most beautiful and resilient, if you honour and mend them with love.

Nothing demonstrates this idea more evocatively than the 16th-century Japanese art of Kintsugi, where breakage and mending of an item of pottery serves to make it more memorable, unique and appealing, as well as nodding to the history and life of the item itself. The practice can be linked to a philosophy of non-attachment, which we can borrow and apply to how we see 'ourselves'. None of us are immutable. We are not one fixed person or way of being, and the world around us certainly isn't predictable or fixed. It doesn't serve us to hold tightly to a status quo or form of being, as change will inevitably come. Kintsugi shows a way to keep the vessel that has been changed or damaged, and to mend the break with something beautiful, like lacquer dusted with powdered gold, rather than attempt to conceal or disguise the 'injury'.

In our lives we will collect fractures, wounds and deep breakages. If we expend vital energy attempting to conceal these perceived imperfections, then we are never showing our ever-evolving true faces to the world we inhabit and the people we engage with. There's also little point throwing the damaged item away: it still works, it just needs a little repair. Better, perhaps, to look to Kintsugi for guidance. We can learn to embrace our broken bits, honour the learning they gave us by mending them with our finest materials, and then show those scars to the world with no shame. It is when we have learned to look at, mend, nurture and respectfully share our damage that we can truly connect with others and live an authentic life.

Your broken bits truly are your superpowers. So why not let them shine?

It's never too late; start right where you are

Maybe you've messed up. You dropped some balls, let someone down, lost a job, partner or opportunity? Perhaps you lost money or missed a deadline, or haven't prepared properly for an upcoming exam, interview or challenge.

You might feel that you have failed and it's all too late. Or that the hurdles you face are too complicated. Or, worse, you've been bereaved, lost your home, or are in some way or other experiencing significant physical or emotional pain.

These are indeed hard things, but they are surmountable. You don't have to wait until something external and beyond your control changes, or to believe that there's no point going forward because it's somehow pointless, or too far gone.

You are going to start right where you are, right now.

Look a little further inside yourself. You want things to be different, don't you? Somehow, in some way, there's a little light inside that desires a change. Find that flame and cup your hands around it. We're going to turn it into a lamp of hope, and you're going to use it to move forward. As slowly as you like, but forward.

Hope: A light in the darkness

Hope is a perpetual warming light in the darkness. It's a light that we walk with and must strive not to lose sight of, especially in the face of the crises that seem to pile up ahead of us as we move forward, globally and in our own personal lives.

We are reminded daily of our impotence in the face of wider adversity, and we can feel very alone, but our individual hopes for a better way forward will lead us into a collective. We will coalesce together on the path towards change with a light that is brighter as a result of all of us pooling our potential. If we give up, then we are in darkness and there is no path — this is the self-fulfilling prophecy of the hopeless.

There is a better way.

We must protect the flames of our 'hope' from the extinguishing winds of the wider world, holding our hands around the light with our heads down as we struggle forward.

Resilient. Determined. Change-makers.

Hopeful vs hopeless

Global news, comparison culture and the endless possibilities that exist in a hyperconnected reality can make us feel endlessly hopeless — that we're not keeping up or achieving what we should.

We need to pull our vision from the macro to the micro. To understand that our hope for individual, material things like a new bag or the latest phone upgrade are not inherently *bad* but could be filling a gap where something else would fit better: perhaps things like security, clarity of purpose, momentum, fulfilment, praise and community. By genuinely connecting with nature, with our work and home communities, and with ourselves, we can find our way back into our relationships and our bodies to feel hopeful again, and to understand that hope will buoy us up on stormy seas once we know what it is we really want to hope *for*.

Often, our feelings of hopelessness can be created by a sense of confusion about what's truly important and by the gradual erosion of our ideals through the relentless bombardment from news and media on every gadget and device we own. We can end up feeling on the back foot, so we throw money, time and effort at things we don't really need so that we can 'catch up'. It feels, and possibly is, hopeless. A constant acquisition of empty possessions and material things may help lift us in the short term, but will fall short in how we desperately hope and crave to feel deep down.

We are bombarded daily by bright lights, clever messaging and the enticing sirens of targeted advertising. It feels impossible to escape from — and it might be easier said than done in today's world — but we need to learn how to disconnect from what we are *told* we want to hope for in life by marketing machines or social media, and instead to tune into what we *do* want.

Once we know, we can steer ourselves, our relationships, our companies and workforces towards that, galvanising us all towards the things that we really want to achieve, and enlisting our resilience and perseverance to take us through all manner of storms to the bright horizons we have set our compass to. We can all hope for happiness, a better workplace, better education, a better world. But we need to be active participants in the journey to get there, using hope as the light when things get rough.

Hope isn't a fanciful, unrealistic and intangible ideal. Far from it. It's the fuel for your fulfilling future.

Part 1
Hope and the
Three Musketeers

1
**Why I
have hope**

I spent most of my twenties and early thirties in deep, chronic pain. The key word here is 'chronic'. Chronic doesn't have an end point, or at least doesn't seem to. It's described in the dictionary as something that 'persists for a long time' or is 'constantly recurring', and my pain certainly was.

Anything chronic seems to be a war of attrition; it grinds you down in its blithe persistence. It is kryptonite to positivity, because it will outlast you if you keep fighting it, and often after the struggle you will only have strengthened and empowered the very thing you are fighting — your own pain. It's hard to stay positive when every time the dust settles after the most recent conflict with your demon, you see that the beast you've fought has just gotten larger and no less powerful.

For me it was physical pain, at least initially. For you it might be heartbreak, loss or emptiness. There's no end of conditions that we humans can experience.

My physical pain was deeply debilitating, and for a very long time I stood in absolute denial of it. Every time pain swung into my field of vision and stared me down, I averted my gaze and focused on a distant horizon of a place I'd like to go, or to an opportunity I wanted to take, somewhere over its shoulder. And then, as I wouldn't take the hint and pain heaved its bulk physically closer and more intimidatingly into my pathway, I'd merely put my hand on its head, my foot on its chest, and vault over it, pretending it was just a momentary block in the road. I was in denial of the 'chronic' aspect, not realising at the time that it wasn't going away. I was using my well-worn toolkit of brute force and ignorance, or — as my dad would say when I'd accidentally rip the buckles or straps on something I couldn't figure out how to undo quickly enough as a child — 'Rip, shred and tear'.

These tactics aren't sustainable though, whatever you're struggling with, and it's a tough road to understanding that something chronic isn't an alien invader or an enemy that is 'other' and can be destroyed. Something chronic is you. It becomes part of you. You are the Trojan Horse *and* Troy, and by killing the invader you will inevitably destroy the host itself. Anger, fighting and rage are understandable when you're faced with a difficult and intractable foe, but they don't always help you in the long run. They're not sustainable or accepting of oneself and of one's situation. They are denial disguised as action, and they are exhausting. Let me talk to you about a different way to see things.

The chronic shift

It takes a resolute decision and a purposeful shift in order to find the chinks of light in a negative situation that appears as stubborn as a mule, whether that situation is your mindset, your physical health, your job, relationship or prospects.

The problem sits there. Recalcitrant. Obstinate. And you have run out of the energy to keep pretending that it's fleeting or momentary, or in no way really *serious*.

Perhaps it's climate anxiety. Perhaps it's your looming exams. Perhaps it's a pervasive difficulty to make good friendships where you feel safe and happy. Whatever it might be that has decided to sit heavily upon you, it becomes clear that it's not just taking a short break before it moves on. It's settled there, sighing, and shifting into ever-more comfortable positions, knowing it won't be leaving any time soon. It is for all intents and purposes 'chronic', and whether the weight of it limits your movement, your breath, your view of the future or all three, it takes resilience, perseverance and self-belief to know that it's worth you staying the course until the beast shifts.

And note that I don't say 'leaves', because we get to a point in this life, some sooner than others, where we realise that nothing ever really leaves us. We are an assimilation of our lived experiences, and it helps to know and accept this. Those things that we see, do and feel are kept somewhere within us, either in our minds, bodies or both, and once we realise we can't excise chunks of our lived and living existence with drinking, over-exercise, workaholism, travel, TV binges or serial romances, we can start finding a way to hold them with some form of loving acceptance, so we can all travel the same road together as a rag-taggle assembly of one. The assembly of you: living, accepting and moving forward to engage with a world that is *also* suffering different forms of chronic pain.

Don't forget also that everything changes. As much as we mourn this and it can break our hearts in so many ways, it is also hopeful. To stay the same is a stagnation, even in the most positive of situations, and for those of us who have suffered (which is to say *all of us*), change offers a fresh dawn and a new day full of promise.

Perhaps therefore, and as evidenced by me, you might like to take this word 'chronic' and repurpose it, applying it not only to negative conditions, but to the opposite. To combat persistent or recurring malaise or pain, perhaps it takes *chronic hope*: the persistent and recurring belief that things will improve, or at least that the ship will slowly turn in the direction you have willed it to, in time.

My path through pain

I was born with my feet turning in. I wore little white casts (that I still have) on my lower legs through the first year of my life to help realign my gait, and I have memories from being a toddler of walking along tabletops in rooms where specialists would look on and eventually nod to approve that I was as fine as I'd be, and their work was done.

My school life was physically fine, some cross-country running, swimming and 1500-metre races in sports events that showed that I could move, even if I had a deep-seated loathing of my own body, for reasons unclear. It was in my early teens that I was ushered up to London for an appointment arranged by my kind uncle, who on observing that my gait was still pigeon-toed and not really aligned, decided it might be good to be checked over. He knew a great clinic near where he lived, where he'd been treated for some back issues himself. My lovely mum and dad agreed, even though they (and I) all felt I was fine. Nothing wrong, no issues, no pain or mobility problems.

Off we went, Mum and me. I didn't want her to come into the appointment, testy teen that I was, and so she sat outside as I entered the room and walked on the treadmill, crimson with embarrassment at having to be in my underwear so the machine could see and track my hip, knee and ankle alignment and the positioning of my feet.

Afterwards, sitting awkwardly in a plastic chair listening to the man explain what he'd observed, I zoned in and out. Now I realise I was perhaps disassociating, my later-in-life ADHD diagnosis making more sense of this, but I zoned back in enough to hear his urgent tone as he described how my gait issues could lead to serious later debilitation. Something along the lines of '... So if you don't get your feet smashed and reset surgically to align them, you'll likely be in a wheelchair at the age of 40 and suffering terrible physical pain.' I zoned out again, nodding.

Those words were terrifying and not anything that made any sense to me, considering my strong frame and general zest for life. So, I ignored them, and didn't tell my mum. I imagine that those all-important findings and recommendations became casualties of the mail, lost between that one-off private appointment in London and my GP surgery at home. At the time, I took the general lack of worry around the topic as a sign that I had probably misunderstood the seriousness of my conversation with the specialist. Surely if it was as solemn as it had sounded, then there would have been more action, some worried and quiet conversation between my parents, or at least some kind of follow-up. But there was nothing beyond my telling everyone that the appointment had gone 'okay', in just the way a young teenager might, when they want the world to go on spinning in the way it always had. The notes somehow never arrived, and we all lived happily ever after in blissful ignorance.

Except I didn't, of course, and then later neither did everyone who loved me and knew how bad it all became. I carried on as usual for years, until sometime just after my mid-twenties when the pain began in earnest. After some years of struggling and the pain cresting into bouts of extreme agony, the process of doctors' appointments, scans and more urgent, pressing action peaked, but with no clear answers it then slowly diffused over time into the medical equivalent of a shrug, a referral to the pain clinic and the general opinion from those 'in the know' that there was nothing they could do, and nothing they could find that was the cause. No one mentioned those little (now large) feet of mine that had been the crystal ball into this future. No one mentioned much in the end, except for rattling larger packets of heavy painkillers and telling me that this was my life now, and the sooner I accepted its limitations and stopped thinking it might get better, the more I would be able to cope with it.

When the incomprehensible instruction to give up hope came from the pain clinic doctor, and before I left the hospital and his care, I asked him why.

'Your hope is getting in the way of your acceptance,' he said. 'If you keep hoping you'll get better, you'll never make peace with where you are. Take the drugs we give you, stop resisting it, and start preparing for your life to change. Apply for a disability badge for your car, consider that you might need to stop working [in my much beloved job as a teacher] and begin to try to accept that sometimes there just aren't any answers.'

As a naturally ebullient person, it had taken a while to register through my optimistic positivity that my situation with my physical pain was grave and needed to be taken seriously. For most of my life until this stage, I'd believed there was nothing bad that couldn't be doused merrily in a sunshiny attitude that everything was probably going to be okay, and then resolutely ignored in the knowledge that it had been dealt with. This attitude included more things than it should have done, from minor issues with friends to major things like physical assault and other trauma.

My issues sat bleached with toxic positivity like white bones in the scorching midday desert sun of my mind. Ossified rather than processed. But for processing, you need mulch, muck and the ability to wade through it, and I didn't have those tools.

It takes time (and perhaps therapy) to learn you need to face stuff for it to get processed, rather than leave all your trauma cluttering up your mind. And it takes making mistakes to realise that this baggage will only trip you up if you haven't faced it and put it away. You've got to deal with your stuff and experience the justified and necessary sadness that comes with difficulties. Sunshine isn't enough to sustain you, especially if you're only *pretending* to be sunny. For me, giving up hope, taking pills and masking the issues in my body without explanation would just be another sun-bleached bone in the graveyard of 'things I didn't solve'. And I wasn't going to do it.

This was a turning point in my life.

When I left that pain clinic, it was with the belief that hope and acceptance could exist *together*. That hope didn't have to mean denial or ignorance; in fact, it could sit with the acceptance of the now and act as a lamp for the path of the future. I could accept I was in pain, that there were currently no answers, that all routes here were exhausted, but I was damned if I was going to assign hope into the bin. I'd accept today and this moment, but then I'd saddle up the hope that things could be different tomorrow.

I would make my hope as chronic as the pain, and see what I could achieve if I kept persevering towards a brighter future.

From pain to Maine

I soon set out on a mission to find other ways to heal myself rather than just relying on pills and giving in. I saved my money from teaching and travelled to different places in the school holidays to try a range of healing methods. Fasting, meditation, yoga and breathwork were some that I found deeply helpful, but also the staples of swimming, Pilates and regular osteopathic and chiropractic care. Everything helped a little, and for a short duration, but nothing 'fixed' me. As soon as I tried to engage back in the hustle and bustle of real life again, my pain would flare up and I would be set back to square one.

It was eventually in Italy, where I had been posted in an educational position by the European Commission and UK Department of Education, that I stumbled on a solution I had never conceived of before. I met a specialist chiropractor who worked with his dentist wife on specifically the kind of problems I was facing. It was while on a desperate visit to his clinic on Lake Como that I first met the man who would offer a solution. He assessed me and announced that the chiropractic treatment I was there for would only fix me for a brief period, because my issue was rooted in the alignment of my jaw. Any speaking, chewing and swallowing after the treatment, he explained, would eventually cause my body to reset itself into torsion, and the predictable pain I suffered would duly return. After some disbelief and shock (this was an entirely new assessment of my condition) I agreed to undergo extensive treatment with fixed braces and other dental interventions to realign my jaw and 'bite'.

Over the course of two years, I improved steadily, with no small measure of fear and disbelief that I would slip backwards again, until I was strong enough to start walking reasonable distances, and sleeping for longer without waking regularly with pain. I then moved to strength-training my weak core and my stabilising muscles, until I eventually began running, then trail running and building confidence in my body for the first time in over a decade.

With my body strong, and my mind ready to explore the world that I'd been on the outside of for so long, I knew I wanted to do something exceptional with my new physical freedom and confidence. So a few years and a few false starts later, I decided to set off and hike the Appalachian Trail southbound: 2,200 miles of footpath through 14 states in the USA. I had hoped for this freedom for so long and now believed I was ready, so I left for Maine, determined to reclaim my wild, adventurous life.

2
Musketeer one: Resilience

After a few days, a monk asked Chopra how he was doing. 'Walking barefoot is painful on these rocky roads,' said Chopra. The monk replied, 'When you walk, the foot on the ground feels pain. The foot in the air feels fine. Focus on that foot.'

A Monk's Journey, Deepak Chopra (adapted)

The quote above is more than apt when sharing one of my own experiences of resilience. It's about a foot, and a failure. Well, I thought it was a failure. Turns out it was a triumph in disguise.

While on the Appalachian Trail, about 1,400 miles in, I had hurt my foot so badly that I knew I was probably going to have to leave the trail. The monk's advice about focusing on the foot that doesn't hurt and that is 'in the air' is all well and good, and I'd used it for a few hundred miles after sustaining my injury, but my foot, ankle and shin were now black and swollen, clicking and grinding with each step, so even the most legitimate and uplifting mental state wasn't going to help me. I was done, and it was time to go.

For anyone this would be hard. For me, it was devastating. I had spent 15 years unable to do anything sustained or physical, and had needed to bow out of nearly every challenge I'd attempted up until this point in my long recovery. And now I needed to bow out again, and not even because of my chronic pain, but because of a busted foot from a slip and kick of a rock weeks before. The utter mundanity of it was galling.

I did go home. I wept and wailed about it, and felt like a failure, but I went. And it was only after returning and healing a little that I realised my resilience. I'd made the correct, safe and best decision for my long-term wellness at a time when all I wanted to do was request stronger painkillers and keep going. I could have pushed through, my willpower would have enabled that, but I didn't. That could be seen as *not* being resilient, that by not going on I wimped out, was weak, or gave up. But *au contraire!* The resilience is in seeing that the game was up for the moment, and keeping the faith in myself that I could come back and finish the trail when I was healed and stronger. The 'bounce-back'. This I did, one month later, after putting my foot up, and I finished my long hike in the wintry December of that year.

Do we understand resilience correctly?

Resilience is described in the dictionary in two ways. These are:

1. The capacity to withstand or recover quickly from difficulties, *or*

2. In terms of an object, to 'spring back into shape'.

In both there is the implied expectation of a 'return to form', indeed *literally* when the object is an elastic band or a sweater in the wash.

Luckily, the expectation of resilience for a human isn't the same. The words 'withstand' and 'recover' don't imply that you need to return to being the same as before or come out of an experience unscathed, merely that you can emerge and be functional. How uplifting not to have the expectation that you should move through life unchanged. And the use of 'or recover' also helps us see that the use of 'resilience' as we can understand it today is much less of the gung-ho, alpha energy of 'never surrender', and much more nuanced, giving room for the opposite of that idea. It gives us space to surrender to failure, defeat, an unexpected turn in the road, or the courage that's needed to say, 'No, I need to stop.'

Often today the use of the word 'resilience', from boardrooms to mountaintops, is rooted around a toxic idea of pushing forward, gritting through it no matter what, never resting, and never letting the bastards grind you down. I don't believe that's helpful. Sometimes the bastards *do* grind you down, and it takes a resilient character to stop, take time out and be able to have enough fuel left in the tank to have another go later or choose a different way. Resilience isn't synonymous with pig-headed stubbornness, but it can often be taken as such.

It's perhaps more helpful to consider resilience as a resilience of our ego. The ability to adapt to challenging circumstances and keep functioning, not seeing the challenges as reasons to beat ourselves up, or to abandon the hope that there's another way to approach the problem.

Learn to bend and flex in the storms of life

Having and cultivating resilience was a large part of how I managed to navigate 15 years of chronic, inexplicable pain and all the mental health challenges that became part of my mercurial journey.

For a long time, my illness felt like I was boxing a wily adversary in a dark room. No sooner had I found my feet and righted myself, a blow would come from a different angle and knock me down again. I became cowed by these often violently painful episodes. There was no clear trajectory of my pain to follow, nothing that I could track and measure to help me predict the flare-ups or the periods of calm, pain-free wellness. Believe me, I tried. From monitoring my sleep, alcohol intake and diet to exploring allergies, inflammatory triggers and every intervention under the sun: nothing provided an explanation for the off/on surges of pain that would leave me sliding down a slope of bedridden depression and physical agony.

I realised that I couldn't keep bracing to get hit by another episode. My baseline pain levels were already very high and my quality of life behind closed doors was low. If I was always tense and expecting another blow, then I would likely break when one eventually came. I needed to step away from the binary thinking of 'I am cured, or I am unwell' to something more flexible. That's where resilience stepped in. The ability to adapt, to expect things not to be stable and be okay with it. In order to make it through, I had to be flexible and ready to shift and cope with whatever was coming next but not be full of fear, which would raise my cortisol levels and exhaust me; to be aware but not alarmed.

To help you to understand what I mean, please try to imagine a time you might have had to balance on unsteady ground. Maybe on a boat, perhaps a ferry? And possibly overnight, like I often did when travelling to France on holiday with my family. As a small girl I'd find the roll of the ferry to be frightening, especially below decks in cabins or corridors, where there were no windows to see or anticipate the swell. I was lucky not to suffer with seasickness, so I'd offer to go and bring back snacks or drinks from the canteen for my parents and sister, and it was there in the long, carpeted halls between cabin doors that I'd see the effect of rogue and unexpected waves on my fellow passengers. A shudder in the hull, a slight flex under my fingertips of the bolts and rivets that held partitions together, and the adults ahead of me would tumble and fall as though an invisible bowling ball had been cast down the passageway.

Not me, though. Dad had taught me well from all his years at sea: don't panic but be aware and ready for what might be coming. So, my little knees stayed bent, my body enjoying the swell and ebb of the sea far below my feet, and when a big beamy wave hit us, I would flex and absorb the impact without stumbling or careening over like a skittle.

I learned, through watching adults skitter and scatter onto the carpeted passages of Brittany Ferries on locked knees and in disbelief that they could be moved by invisible forces, that those who can duck, dive and flex are those who return with the snacks and drinks of life. Those that try to pretend they don't have to adapt to their circumstances, or are rigidly unable to be flexible, are the ones that return empty-handed, with injuries, and food down their front.

The more you lock up and refuse to adapt, the more you get knocked clear over and the more injury you sustain. Resilience would ask that we can adapt both *while* the waves hit us and afterwards: in both the anticipatory phase *and* the post-impact phase. That way, rather than getting knocked clean over, we learn to see in advance when we might need to lean, rest, pivot or duck in order to rally and move forward again.

Resilience involves having a great dollop of this flexible thinking, and enough bounce in your knees to absorb the rogue waves.

So, how do you become more resilient?

Resilience can be built and honed, and it's something we all have the capacity for. Often our early life experiences might help to build an innate ability to be resilient, but it's always possible to start from where you're at.

There are some things that resilient people often have in common:

— Realistic optimism

— Connections with others and a strong social network

— The ability to see moments of opportunity, growth and learning in challenging circumstances

— Flexibility and the ability to adapt to change

My example of being resilient on a physical adventure isn't the only way that resilience can show up in your life. Here are some examples of how being resilient can apply to different situations:

— In the face of, and moving through, fear or phobia

— When changing careers, moving house or switching friendship groups

— When finding love, dating and navigating rejection or disappointment

— Through the process of accepting aging in a way that works for you

— When dealing with grief, or navigating a new awakening of our mortality

— In letting life change without gripping too hard to what 'is' or 'has been'

— When confronted with something overwhelming, like the climate crises, and the sense of helplessness

— When navigating failure, for example in business, education or sport

— Through seeing possibilities in unexpected difficulties

There are endless ways in which a good sense of resilience can support you: it's your ally and a tool to support your growth and ultimately your flourishing. Resilience is not pushing yourself until you break to prove that you tried hard. It's feeling the breath of possibility in the face of disappointment, fuelling the hope that things will be different next time.

3
**Musketeer two:
Perseverance**

What stands in the way becomes the way

Marcus Aurelius

Standing atop Bald Pate Mountain in the heat, feet blistered, hands scratched and my entire body aching, I was in awe of myself. I'd hiked at least 12 miles already, with a pack that was too heavy, up steep slopes and over unforgiving terrain. All in a country that was thousands of miles from my own, and I was alone.

I could celebrate those 12 miles. I could celebrate the next six miles ahead of me. And, when I awoke the next morning, I would feel every inch of my efforts but would recalibrate and begin again for another 10, 15 or 20 miles. Or perhaps it would only be two. The day was yet to tell me, but I would rise and move forward, regardless.

If I had stood atop that same mountain and, while acknowledging my 12 miles, focused instead on the 1,870 miles I had yet to go along the trail to Georgia, then I might have felt entirely different about bothering with the next six, and too defeated and overwhelmed to bother to get up and hike the next day. To persevere, I needed to celebrate the present, acknowledge the small wins and find ways to put one foot in front of another for *just* the mile ahead, no matter the situation. It was only with this focus on the manageable that the unmanageable seemed possible.

Slowly but surely, over the coming months, more than 2,000 miles of trail moved behind me instead of looming ahead.

To persevere means to keep going *despite* setbacks. It's the *action* you take to move forward, underpinned by the resilient mindset you have cultivated.

Perseverance and Resilience are companions, and to do one well without the other is hard.

For me on the Appalachian Trail, my resilience was knowing there was a way forward, and my perseverance showed up as the will to act through each step forward on the trail. I knew when I woke each morning that I would enact the same ritual and routines: stow my gear, pack my tent, filter water, eat a bar, pour coffee granules into my water bottle and shake, bandage my feet, check my maps, and go. Sometimes it rained, for days at a time. Sometimes I was exhausted to the point of collapse. Sometimes I had run out of food and was homesick and angry with the choice I'd made to hike. But every day, I knew that if I just did nothing, then I would sit there in the woods. Deep in the woods. Far from a road, far from comforts and running water to wash in, or a place to sleep indoors.

It was the starkest, clearest reminder that doing *nothing* just keeps you where you are, or sweeps you along to a situation you don't want to be in.

As Hunter S. Thompson said:

And indeed, that is the question: whether to float with the tide, or to swim for a goal. It is a choice we must all make consciously or unconsciously at one time in our lives ... Think of any decision you've ever made which had a bearing on your future: I may be wrong, but I don't see how it could have been anything but a choice — however indirect — between the two things I've mentioned: the floating or the swimming.

I could have stayed where I was on the trail for as long as my food lasted. I might have seen people who passed by. I might have even had conversations and felt like I was part of something, but when everyone had gone past and the day drew in again, I would be in *exactly the same spot* as the day before, just with fewer resources. I knew that on some days, stopping to take a rest day or a break was necessary and part of a bigger plan. But stopping just because I was annoyed? It wouldn't change anything.

So, will you float and end up somewhere worse than where you are now? Or will you start to swim and persevere towards somewhere you *do* want to be?

Have a think about the challenges you are facing now and the perspective with which you're viewing them. Are you trying to take on too much? Is there a big picture that's too overwhelming to tackle head-on? Does the size of it or the time it will take to get there seem insurmountable? It's not. Break it down into hopeful pieces of action and get to it. One piece, one foot, one task and one stumble at a time. Alternatively though, maybe you don't even know where you want to be.

Set your compass

As a first step to feeling lost, if this is you, then lead with how you want to *feel*. The 'doing' is sometimes much easier to figure out when you know if it'll take you towards a desired state of 'feeling'. Do you want to feel more in control? Perhaps more creative? Maybe you want to feel free, or maybe more secure and rooted? Take a moment to create a little mind-map or list of the key feelings you're aiming for, and then you can use that to set your compass to the actions you need to take to get there.

Start, then persevere

What can you do that's manageable today, that will get you moving in the direction you want? Where can you take the tiniest bit of action that starts your wheels turning?

You could:

— Map out your whirling thoughts about the upcoming project onto paper, then cut that paper up and rearrange it so you have a priority list.

— Watch a how-to video on YouTube.

— Do a 10-minute home workout to get your body moving again, no matter how basic or slow it might seem when compared to your longer-term physical goal.

— Call or email the doctor's surgery or therapist and get that first appointment booked in, even if it's a few weeks away.

— Ask someone if they'll help you with that thing you can't do alone — you know, that thing you're avoiding that's stopping the rest of the plan.

— Get up, put your shoes on, open the door and walk for 10 minutes in one direction and then 10 minutes back home. Or more. Even if it's raining. You'll feel better for it. Consider making it a daily routine.

I promise you that once you're under way, it's easier to keep going. Perseverance is the dogged ability to keep doing one small thing, day in day out, towards your goals. To get some momentum, and the only way to start, is to just ... begin.

One step after another

On the 2,200-mile Appalachian Trail, I knew I had to move forward every day somehow. Even a mile was a win (and often even resting in a town to do laundry was moving forward!). Every footstep on a hike is progress; literal, measurable progress on a long trail. You are going forward, and it's not metaphorical as it often is in life when you can't see the goal, or you are not sure why you're 'trying'. On a long hike, you know where you're going, and the only way to get there is to go.

So, resilience told me I could. And my perseverance was in each step. Sometimes joyful and bouncy, often alone bar the trees and birds, but regularly painful and hard-won. But every little step forward was a sign of strength, and each one of those, in a thousand different weathers, moods and mindsets, was what got me to the end of that trail.

Hope lies in your willingness to take that next little step. In the ability to shuffle forward a little more, even when the chips are down and you're exhausted. Hope is the fuel in your tank that powers the perseverance muscle and makes you move. Even when you sometimes don't know why, or *how* you'll ever know why. But with each little step, you are contributing to the fuel that keeps that flame of hope burning and firing up your curiosity for more. For each step takes you to a new angle, a new perspective, a different view through the trees.

Imagine an art class. Twenty students sat in a circle around a bunch of sunflowers. Each instructed to paint. Not only will each artwork be unique to their creator, but even if they had the same style and the same skills, each painting would be different. Why? Because they are all looking at the same thing from a slightly different physical perspective. Sometimes a few inches are all you need to view things differently, and to be able to paint yourself a whole new picture of the future.

Perseverance will always provide progress and perspective. So, go.

And one has to understand that braveness is not the absence of fear but rather the strength to keep on going forward despite the fear.

Paulo Coelho

4

Musketeer three:
Self-worth

> To be yourself in a world that is constantly trying to make you something else is the greatest accomplishment.

Ralph Waldo Emerson

Self-worth is a sense of how much we love, value and respect ourselves. It's our understanding of how much we are worthy of love, belonging and consideration. So many of us, me included, believe that we need to do something to be worthy or valuable, that we must somehow deserve it through our actions, success or achievements. This is just not true.

Your worthiness is intrinsic. You don't have to *do* anything to be worthy. You are already deserving of love, kindness, compassion, encouragement, joy and all the other wonderful human experiences, without you having to change or do anything. You need to begin your worth with you, and *you* need to believe it.

You are enough

I run retreats for confidence and resilience. Whether using the medium of the outdoors, or through writing and creativity, one activity is always the same. At the end of every wonderful residential experience, I hold a ceremony around a fire under the stars.

The culmination of this ceremony involves participants taking it in turns to say one thing they love about themselves to the rest of the group. These people have spent several days together already. They are comfortable with each other, they have done brave and brilliant things outside of their comfort zone during the retreat, they are relaxed and are laughing and chatting merrily in the twinkling firelight. I explain what I'd like them all to do, and they nod and laugh some more, rising with glasses in hand to stand together and begin.

'One thing you love about yourself, in turn please,' I ask.

It seems a simple task. Someone begins. All eyes are on this person: encouraging, warm, and giving expectant smiles of support.

'I love ...'

... which is often as far as each person gets, before quite literally choking on their words or dissolving into tears. They could have waxed lyrical about the person standing *next* to them, but they can't seem to say what they love about themselves.

It's remarkable to see the genuine shock on people's faces as they experience the surge of emotion that comes when they truly try to say something gentle, loving and in praise of themselves. They often cry, and then physically wince and grimace when they finally pull the words up and out into the ether, sharing this thing they love.

The things that get said by these participants are not ground-breaking or wince-worthy. They are things we say to, and about, people all the time. Things like:

— You are so kind
— You're really generous
— You're such a good cook!
— Thanks for being a great listener

— How thoughtful of you!
— You're always putting everyone else first
— Your poetry is beautiful
— You're very funny

However, ask people to switch the pronoun around and say these things about *themselves* and you can see how hard it feels. It *is* hard. Why?

Self-worth. Or, to be precise, our lack of it.

Your self-worth is *yours*. That's the key part of it. It's how *you* feel about *you*. It can't be outsourced, externally validated or reliant on others, and because it's internal and known most closely to you, you can't easily lie to yourself. Somewhere inside, you know exactly what you think of yourself, and often it's pretty rubbish. We can be so cruel to ourselves that we judge ourselves far more harshly, unkindly and unrealistically than any external source ever would. And that is why, when my retreat participants were at their most relaxed and open, it made them choke and cry to say what they loved about themselves. Not because they didn't think they had any lovable qualities — on the contrary — but because in that moment of considering what to say, they realised how unfamiliar it was to look internally in order to praise and not to berate. They were moved because they realised how worthy they actually *are*, and how unnecessarily harsh they had been with themselves.

The shitty committee

So why do we find it difficult to believe that we are worthy? Well, there are endless reasons. We get buffeted and bashed around in life. Between our upbringings, familial relationships, heartbreaks, epic attempts in work and play that lead to crushing failures, humiliations, disappointments, and losses, life can feel pretty harsh at times. And, because we often only focus on the negatives, we set about building a veritable internal smorgasbord of self-inflicted damage from these experiences — and no one ever clears the table, which means we can choose to sample from it any time we like, and often gorge freely in the face of any setback:

— The job you didn't get just proves that you were as stupid as you felt in school that time you were asked to read aloud and messed it up.

— That mistake you made in the accounts is obviously because you're rubbish at maths, just like you were made to feel at 15.

— Your partner broke up with you because [*insert everything you fear and loathe about yourself] and it's all your fault.

— No wonder you didn't get invited, you're not very interesting.

— You didn't get the job because they can see that you'd be useless at it.

— Only 5 of 20 people came to your party because you're not very popular.

— You're late again because you're rude and only think of yourself.

The shitty committee that sits inside our head loves to tell us what we're bad at, and how we've messed up yet again. The incessant mutterings of those cynical old thoughts need to be ushered out to create a new inner dialogue.

It's brilliant to work on yourself, to build your confidence, and create an internal narrative that turns these negatives on their head. How wonderful to think instead: I am good at my job, I am interesting, I am attractive, or I am smart.

These are fabulous things to believe (alongside a little humility and the ability to laugh at oneself, of course). *But* they aren't the solution to having self-worth. These instances of telling ourselves that we did a good job are linked to self-*esteem*, and to pivoting individual moments of self-talk into being more positive. Your self-worth goes beyond that. It is knowing that whether these things are true or *not*, and whether you manage to pivot them or not, *it doesn't matter*, because your value (your worth) transcends any single fleeting moment of feeling good about yourself. Self-worth is knowing you have intrinsic value just as you are, and you are worthy of love, belonging and deserving of hope for a bright future no matter *what* current position or state of self-belief you are in. Yes, even, and especially, right now.

Internal vs external validation

We live in a loud world full of readily available information, and through this, we are constantly confronted with standards that represent a 'successful life' when in reality, this is a highly subjective and individual thing. However, considering our tendency to focus on the shiny input we receive from our screens and the world around us, it's entirely understandable that we can end up becoming externally validated; measuring our worth and value in terms of things outside of us, and in ways that other people believe we should be living. Perhaps we will feel value and worth when we are wealthy enough.

Or when we are seen as successful enough in the eyes of our peers, parents, colleagues or those we aspire to be like.

As the goalposts change with the zeitgeist, we end up flailing around looking for the next thing to hold on to which we can judge ourselves against. This is a losing game, because the goalposts will never stop moving, and through your chasing you'll run out of steam and hope long before you've ever felt solidly grounded in your worth. That's why you need to try to find your worth internally. You need to validate *yourself*. I'm not pretending it is easy, but with a little work you can begin the journey.

Here's a simple thing you can do as you start to wake up to how valuable and worthy you really are: listen to the voices inside, evaluate them, and then kick the old moaners off your shitty committee. In simple terms: look out for your self-talk, and every time you hear something negative, crushing or that puts you down, pause. Challenge that thought, see if it's really true, and then turn it into something more hopeful and positive (even if there *was* a grain of truth in it!). Make it a thought that gives you room to grow as well as acknowledging the bits that didn't go so well. Try it, and I bet you'll weed out some untrue and unhelpful self-talk within an hour of reading this passage.

Remember, it's only you that can change how you talk to yourself. Once you begin to treat yourself with the respect and love you deserve, you'll make darned sure everyone else does too, because you'll know you're worth it.

Part 2
Be captain of your own team

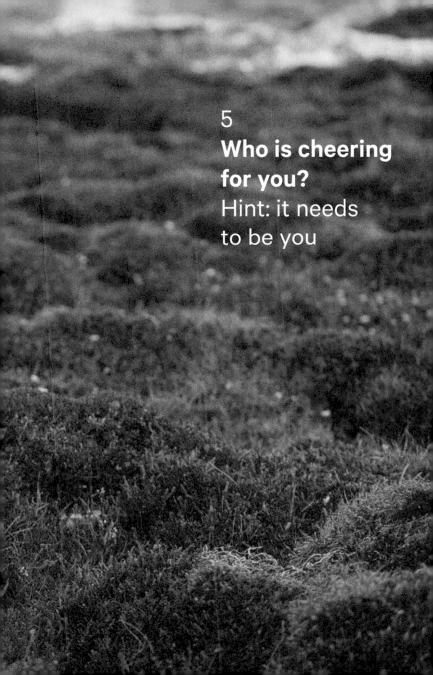

5
**Who is cheering
for you?**
Hint: it needs
to be you

You've got to be captain of your own team.

Nicky Muller: GB athlete, interior designer, and my phenomenal sister

Sometimes you don't know who you are or what you want, and therefore you don't even know what to be hopeful for. Those are hard times, but they are not insurmountable.

There is no one, fixed, version of you. We all change as we grow and move through this life, often positively, but at times we are met with huge problems and curveballs that can come from nowhere. These can derail us and have the potential to make us feel pretty hopeless, especially if we had been using all our hope and energy to move in the direction from which we have become derailed. It could be anything from a bout of social anxiety that means you miss an event you'd been desperately looking forward to, to a redundancy or break-up. I'm sorry if you've been pushed off course recently, it's a blow, and I understand how tricky it is to recalibrate and find the energy to get up and get going again with lightness and positivity. But you're not alone, you're going to be okay, and you can get yourself through it just as steadily as you like.

I was recently diagnosed with ADHD, but at 44 this diagnosis came late for me, as for many others. Although it was a welcome diagnosis, it didn't resolve the difficulties of the life I've already lived. It's been 44 years of trying to fit the square peg of me into the round hole of the world around me. I've wrangled with a raft of issues through my life that I believed for a very long time were because I just didn't *fit*. That despite all my diligent, hopeful efforts I just didn't gel or interface with society properly. This trying, and often failing, to fit in used far more energy than I often had, just to get along.

I also was, and am, a walking contradiction: often enjoying the things that could make me feel so uncomfortable at other times. How to explain this behaviour to others when I couldn't explain it to myself? There was never any predicting when I would suddenly loathe and not be able to cope with a situation I'd so desperately wanted to be in only moments before, like a date, party or a concert. I never had any real understanding about this constant unpredictable dichotomy I existed within, believing myself to be an unreliable judge of my own preferences and constantly doubting my internal compass. I explored formal assessments for cyclothymia *and* bipolar in the years that I was trying desperately to understand the shifting sands that I lived on, both coming back as 'not quite what your symptoms point to, but very closely aligned', and was advised to seek therapy to resolve my ups, downs and the many incomprehensible issues I managed.

Despite juggling so much behind the scenes, I became *so* excellent at the disguise of 'normality' that I was often celebrated and lauded for my ability to succeed in work, to be the 'life and soul' socially and to have many wild, wonderful and often dangerous adventures that I could tell people about, making them marvel and laugh at my bold spirit, courage and ability to hilariously self-deprecate.

I did truly love these elements of myself, even though they came at the cost of the other issues. I liked laughing and making others laugh. I enjoyed adventure, travel, never knowing what I would decide to do next, and I truly loved and was devoted to my work in education. But through so much of it, I wasn't sure who I was, what I wanted or what kind of life I was ultimately building for myself. For every *up* I showed the world, there were downs behind the scenes. Not the usual, metronomic ups and downs of a regular life, but seismic mental valleys and peaks that threw me off my feet as if in a tiny ship on huge swells, never knowing when or how it was going to change. I always wanted to steady the waters, to feel better, to feel more ... peace. I didn't know how to attain those things because I didn't know how to want them more than I wanted the dopamine-spiking behaviours that I had been hunting for years without realising why. I was constantly changing what I wanted, getting in my own way, and knocking myself off the path I was trying so hard to navigate. I wasn't able to be true to myself, because I didn't really know myself.

Perhaps that concept sounds familiar?

You don't need to have ADHD or any other neuro-development difference to relate to the idea of not knowing yourself, of not being truthful about what you are, what you love or who you want to be. I think most of us can struggle to cheer for our full 360-degree selves. I use the ADHD example because it's one that I know, but I've coached and taught enough people to know that the variations on this theme are endless. The shame, embarrassment, fear, loneliness and self-loathing we can carry from not being true to who we are or what we want our lives to be is crippling for most of us on some level or another.

For me, ultimately, I couldn't hide the mess of my life any longer, and it was the best thing that could have happened to me because it allowed me to bring all the bits of me to the surface and for me to *have to* make sense of them and finally, with help, join them together into a full, visible person.

It also allowed my sister's deeply helpful advice of being 'captain of your own team' to properly resonate and make sense to me, finally. If you're not even sure who's on the team, and they're not even all showing up at the right time, how can you guide, lead and encourage them properly? If you don't know what you're truly hoping for or what you hope to achieve, then how can you take yourself in that direction? You must get your shadow-selves (those parts of ourselves we hide from others) and all those true elements of your desires and dreams to step out onto the field in full view, because team training only works when the whole team shows up.

Are you masking?

I realised that I hadn't only *not* been cheering for myself, but for the longest time I'd been *fighting* myself — the very thing I had taught myself not to do with my physical pain. I hadn't even realised that I'd been so unkind to the struggling elements of my psyche because I'd relegated them behind masks of 'ordinary' for so long, telling them to dance to the tune that I believed I needed to play to get by in the world.

You'll find any amount of late-diagnosis ADHD folks who will tell you about the grief they experience when they receive diagnosis (after the initial elation), because there comes a moment when you look back at your life so far and wonder which bits of your personality are you, and which bits are coping mechanisms to fit into a world that wasn't going to accommodate your quirks, or deal with your difficulties. Perhaps, you realise later, the world was not even directly rejecting you, but it was clear to me from a very young age that there are ways to thrive and fit in, and ways to get turfed out of the pack or rejected.

Whatever it is you've been hiding, coping with or playing down, don't beat yourself up for it. We all cover up and conceal in the hope that it'll help us belong. Perhaps it's a deep-seated part of our ancient brains that tells us we need to mask up and fit in so that we're not cast out of the group and left to fend for ourselves on the plains? Whatever it is, many of us pull on the cloak of 'normal' to get by, until we can't anymore. At some point the tricky elements that make up 'you' come tumbling out of the cloak, strewing your issues on the floor for all to see, and you have to sort it out.

Don't worry — it's actually a great relief.

We can believe that these issues we carry and manage for years will fade, as the distance and time between us and them increases. In my experience that's not the case. Sometimes it feels as though distance may *indeed* make the issues we carry get smaller, but they somehow seem to also get *heavier* as they reduce in size. Our issues and fears from the past become tiny pinheads that contain the weight of universe: ever more exhausting to carry with us as we go forward. It's okay to find ways to stop at any age and bring them to the surface and resolve them, assimilating them into our 'world-facing' self. It's also okay if they all spill out at once and cause a bit of a mess, like they did for me. It means that you can begin to know yourself, and in doing so, you can learn how to treat all parts of yourself better. Your hope that you and your life can be different in the future can feel authentic and honest because you are learning exactly who and what is on board your team.

The journey into self-knowledge is a lifelong adventure, so don't expect to complete the mission, but as long as you're trying to learn and assimilating more understanding as you go, that's *more* than enough to be proud of. Then, with your growing self-awareness, you can cheer yourself on towards all that you hope for.

Self-doubt and not getting in my own corner has caused me all kinds of trouble. But as I've spent time really tackling and learning about the things I struggle with, and the things that make me a bit 'different', I've become less likely to beat myself up and more inclined to see mistakes and problems as learning opportunities, being kind to myself when I screw up. And remember, screwing up happens to us all sometimes, and at all different ages.

I learned that it's okay that the way my brain works makes me seem different to other people. I'm owning it. It's okay to ask for help, even if it feels hard. It's okay for me to struggle, repeatedly, and still hope that next time it'll be different. It's okay for you to do those things too.

Ebullience around the idea of hope isn't silly or naive, it's just us carrying on fiddling with things under the bonnet and being positive that things can keep improving. There is no one 'moment' where everything comes together and there is no perfect place to reach where problems cease entirely. Living well and in alignment is an ongoing job, and an ever-evolving process of getting to know yourself as you change and grow.

That's why hope is so important — it keeps you moving forward. Because just as there's no one solution, there's no one single 'failure' that takes you back to square one either. No matter how much you believe this recent problem has 'ruined everything'. It hasn't. Every stumble is a lesson, and every success is happy information for further growth. Every time that your hopefulness picks you up and moves you forward, you're closer to where you want to be. Don't let anyone try to convince you there's no point in continuing to make adjustments, because every day and every bit of learning counts.

You'll get there.

The hackneyed saying about the definition of insanity being where you 'do the same thing repeatedly but expect different results' doesn't apply when you're tweaking the 'thing': the thing being how you see and understand yourself. When you're improving the component parts, why shouldn't you try again to be hopeful for a different outcome for yourself?

When I tried to align with others and 'be like them', it didn't work. I wasn't being myself, so I stood out as an imposter or fraud, even if only to myself. I was trying to be a me that I wasn't. So, I embraced my differences, my difficulties and my true self, and then I began to watch myself shine. I began leading myself forward from an authentic place and could really get behind it. I was truly being captain of the team I led: personally, in work, and in life. And because I'd tuned in to my real me, I was also aligned with the team around me — friends, family, co-workers, my potential, my true hopes and dreams — who had been cheering for me all along but whose encouragement and belief in me hadn't before married up with my own for myself.

When what you believe about yourself aligns with what your subconscious and your cheerleaders already know about you, you're unstoppable.

So, stop hoping to be someone else. Instead, embrace who *you* are and then start moving your whole team towards your goals. Here's how ...

Find out what makes you tick

Perhaps you find these ideas out of reach or a little overwhelming. That's understandable, as we're *always* learning about who we are. It's not a one-and-done process, and it's also not something that needs to be terrifying or take a 'falling apart at the seams' moment to happen. Getting to know who you are so you can captain the team of 'You' and feel authentic hope can be as gentle and slow as you need it to be.

Start learning about yourself. Not the *you* that you wear every day to get work, family or social life sorted, but the quieter parts of you that have had to take a back seat for a while.

What are your values? What makes you feel aligned and good, or grounded and strong? Observe your reactions to things in your daily life, the way you see others or yourself behaving, the things that make you feel light and optimistic (or, dare I say it, hopeful) and also note the things that bring up a coil of distaste or disquiet before you push them quickly back down through habit.

Take note of the flutter in your chest or the tickle in your gut. See what makes your dial move — your gut will tell you a great deal if you let it. In practical terms, it's really helpful to keep a log: a note, a diary of 'You' and what you really love. Where is that trail of breadcrumbs taking you? Learn to recognise, record and then embody your core values that you may be reacquainting yourself with or learning for the first time in a long time. Buy a little notebook and keep it close by in your bag, office or home so you can grab it and record those little moments of feeling alive, and bit by bit you'll be building your bank of treasured remedies for when you feel lost or disconnected.

When hope is a stranger, and you feel like you don't even know *what* to hope for anymore, you need to come back to these flutters in the chest, the stirrings of joy, and the values you feel aligned with. Make sure to book in a 'spiritual' physiotherapy appointment with yourself to ensure you're not moving the body of your life in a direction that's at odds with these values and those things that really light you up. If you're moving against them then you'll know because it'll cause pain — first emotional or mental, then at some point physical. Which one will you listen to when it shouts at you, and how long will you ignore the noise of body or mind? A long time, as I did? Or will you move swiftly to the instruction that comes from within? The feeling of unease in your mind or the aching bones, physical exhaustion, malaise and nausea of your daily grind are really one and the same.

Think about the following elements as examples of things that can show who or what is on your team. Are they the right ones and really representative of *you*? You're the captain, you're in charge, and if you don't love how your team presents, then you can change it.

Does your team feel right?

Maybe you haven't had the chance to pause and take stock of how you're living recently, or considered how your choices are having an impact on the way you feel. I encourage you to stop and take a look. Use the list below to help. Do these things best represent your best 'you'?

— The people you socialise with

— The work you do

— The relationship you're in

— The clothes you wear

— The place you live

— The things that look like success to you (when you've 'made it')

— The friendships you cultivate

— The energy you put into the community you live in

— How you show up for those who are important to you

Are they you? Or are they echoes and imprints of school, or your parents who told you that what you liked wasn't good enough? Are they just ways of living, and things to have, that society tells you that you *should* have? Or have they been tools of survival that don't really represent you.

If you can, look inside and try to begin the process of marrying what's there with what you show the world, and lead yourself kindly forward.

Why don't you take a second to try this now?

Grab your notebook or a scrap of paper:

1. **Write down 3–5 things that you like about yourself.**
   Your generosity? Your new hair? Your ability to fix anything? Get it down, don't be shy. Once you have these things on paper, ask yourself if you get to use, flex and show these qualities and skills enough in your life. If not, how can you use and show your favourite bits more in the day-to-day?

2. **Write down 3–5 things that made you feel good lately.**
   The sun on your face as you sat in the car after work? The song you heard in the coffee shop that you haven't listened to for years? The feeling you got when you wrote a poem for your friend's birthday? Find the things, and then ask yourself what it *was* about these things that made you feel so good. Were you taking a moment to relax and be present? Were you helping others? Were you tapping into your creativity for the first time in ages? Whatever it is — do more of that.

You try to know yourself and then you *must* cheer for yourself. You must captain your team towards having your best life, and to make that happen you need to know and accept *who* you are. Then you can authentically, vocally and proudly lead yourself towards your future feeling strong about your goals, because you'll know they're authentically linked to *your* values and *your* core purposes. And they're all led by a strong captain: you.

6
Failure is a gift

> A gem cannot be polished without friction, nor a man perfected without trials.

Seneca

The tagline of this book says, 'Why you should never give up'. It's direct, isn't it, and maybe a little judgemental sounding? Well, perhaps, until you consider that giving up *isn't* synonymous with changing your mind or failing. To give up means to give up on *everything*, even on hope.

Every option is, of course, yours for the taking. These range from becoming completely apathetic, to taking never-ending duvet days or sobbing into your sleeves. Sometimes life really does come at you like a series of blows, leaving no time to breathe between the punches. You might feel like giving up, but having the wherewithal to consider the logic of doing so means you haven't done so yet. There's a road ahead. This road can often seem littered with difficult obstacles, unhelpfully labelled with words like 'fail', 'quit' and 'unsuccessful'. I'd urge you to reconsider what these words really mean, and try to embrace them as teachers and guides, barring your way from wrong turnings and bumpy roads that won't serve you.

What if every time you didn't succeed you were *actually* being redirected to a new piece of learning, or the empathy, insight and humility that will help pull you and others out of some tight spots down the line?

What if they're the artist's chisel, shaping you into the person you're becoming? What if you gave up *just* as the best piece of wisdom was being gifted to you but in a language you weren't familiar with?

Different lens, right? Try it.

Quitting

I'm a big fan of quitting. I don't know why it's got such a bad rap. A quitter is simply someone who has recognised what doesn't serve them and has the confidence and courage to say 'no'. They walk away even when they don't know what the other options are yet. In fact, that which looks the most reckless can often be the most necessary, life-changing step towards hope. The hope that you deserve better, that there are things out there that are the *right* path rather than the one you're on that doesn't work. There's bravery in quitting.

How to quit

Of course, there are *ways* to quit. I think it absolutely matters how you do it. Kindly, considering others as much as you can, with honesty and authenticity. It's very hard to argue with someone's heartfelt honesty, so if you need to quit the relationship, the job, the adventure, the friendship, the business or the team, then do so with integrity. This way you *may* quit, and that can feel hard, but you'll always be able to look back and know you did a tough thing in the most admirable way you could.

As we age and move through life, there isn't one of us that doesn't begin to recognise the complexity of living.

Of being overwhelmed, having painted oneself into a corner, having said yes when we should have said no, gone when we should have stayed, said what someone wanted to hear rather than what we really *meant*, and carved whole scenes of destruction through our sheer human fallibility. We all see things through different lenses as we grow, and it makes us more forgiving of others, and hopefully of ourselves. Still, if you quit, leave, throw the towel in, break up, resign, then do it well. It's nice to have healthy quitters to look up to as we rehabilitate the concept!

After I had hiked the Appalachian Trail, the South West Coast Path and the West Highland Way, all past the age of 40, I figured that I was ready for more. In the confinements of Covid, I had written a book, and it was scooped up in short order by a fantastic agent and then publisher. Fabulous. But I'd spent most of the time that I could have been writing the book, sitting, and imagining the great outdoors that I was barred from. Yearning to be out there, to use the working body that I had reclaimed.

As each little travel plan was whittled away from me, I felt more rebellious. My Pacific Crest Trail permit for 2,800 miles in the US? Useless now. Hike cancelled. My flight to New Zealand after the PCT to hike the Te Araroa? In the bin too. So, I planned bigger in rebellion. I would hike the Continental Divide as soon as I was allowed to travel to the US, and as soon as it was okay and within the sensible seasonal hiking window.

The Continental Divide is a 3,100-mile wild trail down the spine of the USA. It's a mammoth hike in some of the most remote and stunning parts of the country, walking through lands owned by grizzly bears and mountain lions, weeks spent far from civilisation. I knew that *this* would make me feel less weak and contained. This was what I needed to continue to prove my body was fixed, that it worked, I was a trailblazer for those with chronic illnesses. If I wasn't planning to go harder and more perilously into my future, then I wasn't progressing, was I? Well, I was wrong. I thought I was ready, but I wasn't. That's not the key takeaway though. I thought it was what I *wanted* ... but it wasn't.

So, I dodged around all manner of obstacles to get to the southbound head of the Continental Divide Trail. I flew from the UK to Cancun, waited out 15 days of quarantine in Mexico, entered the US and travelled by sleeper train from Seattle to Glacier National Park. It was exhausting, all the while clinging to the belief that this was going to be a way to raise my stock again, to show what I could do. From Glacier we drove for hours into true wilderness; the only road there led north, across the Canadian border. It was closed still because of snow, but our guides got us there. Blackfeet tribe 'trail angels', who had driven us up, told of their frustration and pain that arbitrary borders bisected their flow across ancient territories, imparted their wisdom and blessed us with tobacco. I was further from any feeling of security than I've ever been, surrounded by elements and animals that made me quail at their stark, ferocious beauty, all because I had obstinately placed myself out on the furthest circle of my comfort zone. I could feel the axis wobble and splinter, but I was too far out and too committed to step off with any grace. If I was coming off, it was going to be because I was thrown. Or so I thought.

I didn't know it then, but undiagnosed ADHD, altitude sickness, my level of fitness and anxiety after months in Covid isolation, my hiking speed, and huge hormonal fluxes were going to conspire against me. I was going to undertake a short, brutal and very beautiful hike, hear of a woman killed by a grizzly, ugly-cry with frustration, snap with humiliation, feel every day of my age and eat every morsel of humble pie before I did what was actually right for me. Before I finally made peace with letting go of the 'I should', and I quit.

I quit and watched younger, lither, fitter hikers breeze on with confidence and full tanks. I quit and didn't even have a physical injury to point to as the reason. I quit after telling thousands of Instagram followers that I was going to hike the CDT, after leaving my partner at home and our relationship imperilled because of it. I quit even though I had spent a huge amount of money to be there. I quit because I hoped that it was the right risk to take.

And when I was honest about it, spoke it out loud and shared it with friends, it all rang true. It was the best quit I could have quitted. From there, I undertook a wild series of mini-adventures that included riding motorbikes, taking an unplanned ferry to Alaska to journey into Denali, and hiring a car to drive all around the west coast of the USA with no fixed plan.

This trip culminated with a long, exhausting drive to the giant redwoods of northern California, a few motel rooms, and eventually a huge crash of body, mind and soul somewhere in a dusty, drought-blighted field in Portland, Oregon. Shortly afterwards, and close to full breakdown, I quit my journey entirely, departed the US and came home to seek support and, ultimately, a diagnosis of ADHD, and some longed-for answers.

It was a tough road to travel from that big hopeful dream to the crummy realisation that I couldn't do it and was having to go home. I'd been there before though; we all have in one way or another. All you can do is realise that it's *not* giving up. Giving up would be forgoing your intuition that things need to be different. Giving up would be going on. I know, it sounds strange, doesn't it, but don't you feel better about something right now this very moment, if you view your previous 'giving up' with this new perspective?

Embrace the quit

Failed attempts at anything are the scraped hands and knees of adulthood tree-climbing. Where's the fun in being able to shimmy up the tree of life without the bumps and bruises that chart the pathway of your learning, showing the well-earned and hard-sought route to the vast views at the top?

You see, 'The Quit' will take you to the places you need to go, if you're courageous enough to engage its services. It's a hopeful action, one that propels you forward, sometimes more violently than you'd like, throwing you up or down so fast that your vision blurs and you feel sick. Sound the alarm! Pull the lever! Embrace the quit. And then let your hope for better things roll out the new path in front of you.

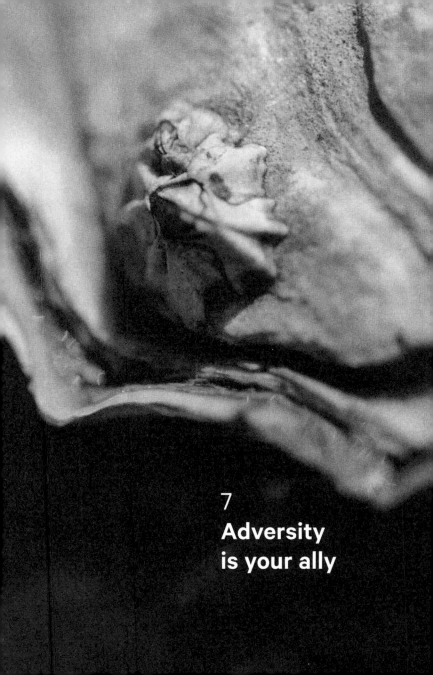

7
**Adversity
is your ally**

Having nothing to struggle against, they have nothing to struggle for.

Charles Bukowski

We all come up against problems in life and, when we do, we often hear that we should 'fight' these obstacles in our paths.

Any adversity that we are presented with, be it in the workplace, on a project, in a relationship or even in our own bodies, it's often commonplace to use this vernacular to show how we are making efforts not to let the negatives of the situation win out. 'She is fighting cancer' or 'He's battling not to lose his job'. I understand why this advice is given, but the use of the word 'fight' isn't helpful in my experience. However, back when I was suffering the most, I wasn't any different: I was battling too. For me, and for a very long time, I would be 'fighting' chronic pain. Determined not to let it win, not to let it cross my ever-shrinking frontiers and pillage my energy, friendships, aspirations and talents.

I thought this was the right thing to do, of course: when you are engaged with an adversity you can't let it in through the front door, can you? You can't sit back and observe it or let it do as it will without pushing back. For your own sense of self-worth, you should tackle it head-on and show yourself and the world around you that you've not given up.

Fight. Tackle. War. Battle.

But if your language is combative, disheartened and heavy, you will naturally see more of what you believe to be real. You'll *feel* the struggle, you'll know that you're battling. This doesn't help you feel better; it actually drains you further because these are words that, by their very nature cause the fight-or-flight system to activate, to encourage adrenaline and cortisol to flow and to get you ready to take on a challenge. You might think that this is beneficial, but what's the outcome if you aren't successful that day, on that occasion, with that pitch or in that boardroom? Words like lost, failed, defeated and weak. This language isn't conducive to feeling hopeful, to chalking it up to a good try and learning lessons to take forward to the next time, a step towards growth and understanding.

Especially when, like me, the only person you're fighting is yourself. I suffered such debilitating chronic pain that my fight to 'beat it' only exhausted me further. I was using vital energy to fight myself. There's no winner in that equation. So, I stopped using that language and started viewing adversity differently.

I made friends with it.

I was starkly reminded why it was right for me to do so when observing one of my students, who suffered from a variety of challenges and struggled to manage tackling them. He had diabetes (type 1) and Asperger's, as well as issues with defiance and following instructions. So, I witnessed him sometimes eating much more sugar than he should to 'dominate' his diabetes and show that it wouldn't control his life. This was shocking and curious to me. His diabetes was part of him. It *was* him, so fighting it and challenging it was only fighting himself. His blood sugar would soar and make him feel deeply unwell, and in the long term could cause damage to his eyes, kidneys and nervous system. Yet so strong was his desire to fight his condition that he would regularly battle his own body down in the process.

This is a stark and extreme illustration of how we can be the opposite of our own team captains. We are the front line of our own emergency services, so the least we can do is basic first aid with our language and thoughts.

Bring the wolf inside

With a little practice and a pivot of perspective, it is *absolutely* possible to see adversity as your ally and teacher. To see that which gradually drains you of hope like a small hole in your bicycle tyre as the reason to get off the bike and set about learning how to fix it. It might sound trite, but it's possible.

Consider whether you can make friends with your adversary, whatever it might be. When I embraced my chronic pain as my friend, it calmed down. As my system let go of combat and fear of loss, of gripping white-knuckled to a 'win' and perfect health or being pain-free, my body had space to see what it was actually feeling. It was the equivalent of putting down my weapons on the front line and stepping out of the trenches into no-man's land to play football and break bread with my pain.

Once your adversity has shown you your limits, you can work within those limits and help improve your situation. Instead of blindly wrestling my body up and out for a long walk after fistfuls of painkillers, I swallowed instead my pride, and asked my pain what it was able to do that day. This meant that instead of a 10k coast walk we might do a 2k stroll to the beach and back. When I'd been 'fighting', the 10k option would have made me feel victorious and jubilant momentarily, but then bereft and defeated when I couldn't walk that evening and had to cancel things over the next few days — back to square one again. But for a 2k walk, I managed to see people on the way, speak to friends, socialise, enjoy my time in the elements, return home feeling accomplished and know that the next day my body would feel fine, and that next time we could perhaps do 2.5k. It seems simplistic, but you'd be amazed how many of us are stuck in a loop battling the things we think are our key enemies, when really, we just need to bring the wolf inside and work within limits that both can find achievable.

What if, instead of feeling utterly discouraged and hopeless because you didn't get the promotion you applied for, you asked what it was that held you back, had the grace to listen to critique and used that to help you hone key skills for the two or three other positions you apply for (and get) when you're truly ready?

What if, instead of feeing hopeless and overwhelmed when you see trash along the roads, plastic on the beach and read about global climate disasters, you instead put on some gloves, bought a litter picker, and filled a bag with trash to put in the bin when you go out on your daily or weekly walk? You can't fight the world. You can't change huge problems overnight, but you absolutely can bring that adversity in and ask what it needs from you. It needs you to help, and by clearing your local trail, the edges of a car park, school lane or hedgerow, you're befriending the issue and making a tangible and empirical difference. You feel invested and involved, and that is galvanising. Your energy is spent not on sleepless nights and despair, but instead on setting an example to those who see you, leading others to do the same, and building community around a problem. Making the abstract fear a concrete, solvable and manageable task, which will all add to the solution of the whole.

Something is *always* better than nothing.

— A walk instead of a run if your knees hurt

— Volunteering when you can't afford a ticket

— Helping someone for just 20 minutes rather than not showing up at all because you are too busy

— Seeing age as a gift of wisdom and experience rather than a handcart to the grave

Adversity will come as surely as the sunrise and the tides. There is no ducking or avoiding it. Fighting the tide will exhaust only you, not the ocean. So, see it for what it is: part of the ebb and flow of living. As your teacher with lessons in hand. Negotiate the best way through for you both and turn that adversity into a building block to step onto, taking you ever closer to your goals.

Part 3
How to use hope to fuel your tank

8
**Find the gold
under your feet**

**All that is gold does not glitter,
not all those who wander are lost;
the old that is strong does not wither,
deep roots are not reached by the frost.**

The Fellowship of the Ring, J.R.R. Tolkien

I was recently in the Sahara Desert, assisting on a charity trek. I had never hiked in such huge and arid terrain before and had many interesting conversations with the local guides as the days went on.

I was particularly interested in water, and the perceived lack of it. How could anyone ever survive out here, where there was nothing but stunning dunes and beautifully sculpted, rippling golden sand under the blistering sun? They told me that, should I pay closer attention and think logically, I would be able to source water.

'Look around,' one man said. 'Can you see anything growing?'

I scanned the horizon across 360 degrees of hot, baked distance and began to take note of some trees, seeming to grow out of the side of a dune, with nothing else for acres around them. And some small shrubs growing in another tatty cluster in another area. These weren't lush green oases with palms and pools next to them, they were dusty and brown, with darkened leaves that blended into the landscape.

'There!' I gestured over towards the trees. 'Over there are some trees, but no water to drink.'

They laughed kindly. 'Of course, there is no water ready to drink. You must look a little harder, then do a little work. The water is there, it just isn't obvious. You need to use the logic that the tree must find water, then so can you.'

And then they proceeded to explain how I would, if stuck, need to dig deep holes around any vegetation then sit back and wait. If nothing happened, then dig deeper, down towards where the tree roots must stretch. Eventually, water will begin to seep into the bottom of the hole you have dug, and you can drink.

There is always something to quench your thirst for better days, even when the terrain of your life seems purely arid on the surface. You just have to use some tools, dig a little and be patient until you can see the energy, possibilities and potential seep in. Just because opportunity isn't presented to you on a plate with a label and a bow, it doesn't mean it's not there. Sometimes the things you most wish and dream for are right in front of you, under your nose ... you just hadn't noticed.

The deeper that sorrow carves into your being, the more joy you can contain.

The Prophet, Kahlil Gibran

9
Tools
To help you see
what you have,
so you can get
what you want

This chapter is about taking stock of where you are and seeing the good that's right there. Know that you have enough in the tank to get through this period, even if you need to dig deep for it, and that any challenges you are facing will help you appreciate the better times that are coming.

The tools you find in the worst of times will always be useful later on, especially when you need to build some reserves of hope for the better times ahead.

Here are some ways to find a little hope when you feel lost:

1. Listen to someone else's story

Look to someone who has found hope in dark times and come through, perhaps against insurmountable odds. One book and figure I've looked to for this in the past is Viktor Frankl's *Man's Search for Meaning*. It describes his experiences in the Nazi death camps and how he survived not just physically, but spiritually. It's a humbling read, and the essence of his message is that we cannot avoid suffering, but we *can* choose how we cope with it, and can find lessons and meaning in our suffering that spur us on. That meaning, in turn, gives us purpose. And purpose is vital to our happiness and movement forward. It's also quite simply an incredible book for putting your problems into a different perspective.

A little closer to home, I often draw on the experiences and conversations I have had with students I teach and have taught. Through my (now 20 years!) of working in education around the world, I have taught many different young folks from hugely diverse backgrounds, nationalities and socio-economic situations. Irrespective of their differences, there are often many things that are similar about these young people, and one is that they rarely give up. They might rail against authority, grump, swear, fight, refuse, scream, throw things, become withdrawn and silent or *say* that they are done and giving up, but it's actually very rare. Their inherent sense of hope, unless deeply damaged, is a flame that keeps burning and that roars with heat when given the right oxygen.

It's been such a privilege to have had the opportunity to show them they have their own oxygen, and that they just need to find the right dial to turn in order to release it onto their flame. I've seen students managing huge flux and trauma find the courage and resilience to trust me, and then in turn trust themselves. I've watched them use the tools I've shared to take themselves out of whatever situation they have been in, and not give up.

2. Find a micro purpose
(if the macro is too hard right now)

As has been said many times, 'Be the change you want to see in the world'. If you want to be more hopeful, find something to *do* that brings some hope, and if not for yourself then for someone else. Take a walk (a positive action in itself), but set the goal of picking up five or ten pieces of litter on your walk. That's a purpose — you are taking some weight from the back of Mother Nature, you are paying back to the walk you are enjoying, and you are making it a more lovely place to walk for those who come behind you. As you put those pieces of litter in the bin, realise that you just made a positive change in the world — something tangible, practical and useful. You could perform a number of these little actions each day and you will be pouring positivity into the community around you in your own, micro, way.

You can't fight the news, the large environmental issues the world is facing, and you can't fix big economic problems, of course, but don't let these things freeze you in your tracks and overwhelm you. It's easy to feel hopeless when you look at the huge picture, but you can feel hopeful and galvanised at a micro level when you take meaningful action in areas you *can* control and affect. These micro actions add up, and they matter. They will help feed into a larger picture of hope and momentum for you.

3. Something is always better than nothing

Don't have the energy to apply for a new job? Then watch a YouTube video about learning a new skill that you can discuss when you do have the energy and you get the interview.
No juice to go for a run? Then go for a walk instead.
Don't have time for a walk? Make it 10 minutes even in the rain, you'll feel better. When you're feeling a bit low and hopeless, your brain will tell you there's no use in *anything* if you can't do it like you used to, or run as far as you did before, or can't finish it. Don't listen — it doesn't matter. Just begin. Read a page. Write a page. Tidy one drawer rather than the whole room. Begin and tell yourself it's only for 10 minutes and see where that takes you. Something is *always* better than nothing, and nothing is too small compared to zero.

4. Watch the sun come up

Yes. Even if it's early. Set your alarm, find a spot where you can sit with a favourite beverage and watch the sun rise. Or go for an early morning walk and watch it. The sun comes up every day, and each time it does is a chance for you to reboot and start again. It's possible to begin again at any moment, of course, but there's something symbolic and beautiful about seeing the new day begin, to hear nature begin to wake up before the rest of the world does, and to be part of that fresh beginning where anything could happen.

In a world where things happen to us every day, why couldn't today be the day that something good and wonderful happens for you? Or you could just welcome a day with no expectations or pressures. Whatever kind of day it is going to be, you're seeing it begin — fresh and new.

5. Good old gratitude

Being grateful for things involves first identifying the good things we have so that we can then feel gratitude for them. Just this simple act means that we shift our gaze away from 'lack' and towards a more positive appraisal of our situation. It's true that gratitude is a superpower, however it's also true that we can be cynical beings, and no matter how many times we might have heard the benefits of recording our gratitude in a diary or journal, we might think it's a little clichéd. Well, it's hackneyed because it's true. And even though you've heard it a million times, are you actually *doing it*? Did you *try it* for more than three days?

Give gratitude journalling another whirl around the dance floor and try to do it without a preconceived ironic 'detachment' that makes you feel a bit above it somehow but doing it anyway. That's a waste of time. Commit to being grateful beyond a thought in your head for, let's say, 30 days. Write it down. Do it every day. It could be one thing a day but it's likely to be more, and I promise it's worth it and you'll feel the difference in your outlook pretty fast.

6. Contemplate the seasons

Everything has its time. Things fall back in winter, storms break limbs from trees, leaves drop, frost petrifies everything in its path, and all appears stagnant and lost. But you know it's not the case, and you know that the same applies to your state of mind and current situation too. The sun warms the earth again in due course, shoots spring anew, wounds on trees where branches have been lost in great winds heal to form beautiful patterns and scars that show the beauty of healing and adaptation.

Learn to have patience with the seasons of your life. Accept the darker, colder days of your winters and be reassured that you have seeds and acorns enough stowed in burrows and around the roots of yourself to make it to spring. You will flourish yet, and so will the world around you, and you will be grateful for the lessons of resilience and perseverance learned in your dark and earthy seasons.

7. Laughter

Find something or someone that makes you laugh. You might feel a bit resistant to this at first — a lower mood and feeling a bit hacked off can make you feel less likely to want to find things to laugh about, but try sticking on an episode of your favourite sitcom or clip of a standup comedian or even better, go to a comedy gig. Studies have shown that humour and laughter can actively improve people's state of hopefulness. Laughter can help suppress negative thoughts and replace them with more uplifting and positive ones, which might not solve whatever problem you are facing, but it *can* give you some mental space and flexibility to see your situation a little differently and nudge you towards some motivation to seek different pathways forward.

8. Goals and pathways

After reading this book, my hope is that you understand the importance of knowing yourself. Once you do, you are better able to set goals that you really do want and feel motivated to move towards.

This is the first part of cultivating a strong sense of hopefulness — a purpose or goal to achieve. Then, working backwards, you need to have the *drive* to achieve those goals. This should be simple if you've been authentic because you've chosen goals based on real desires, so you will be intrinsically motivated to achieve them, rather than extrinsically motivated by a need to please others or fit in, which give little agency.

With the goals, drive and agency in hand, your next step is to create pathways to achieve the goals. Not just one, but multiple. Imagine many different routes you could travel along to get to where you desire to be. Some might be contingent on parts of other routes being successful, and some might be stand-alone, but the very creation of multiple pathways and thinking through how they could work will give you hope, as it will become clear to you in an empirical and concrete manner that these goals are achievable.

Not only that, but when you have multiple ways of achieving something, you build your capacity for resilience, because you see that failure on one pathway isn't a finite situation: it's not a failure of the whole. You can jump pathways or adapt and create new ones. You can *persevere* because you know it's not fruitless to do so. You have a direction, and you just need to keep moving forward step by step towards the goal. Once you stand back and see there's more than one way to achieve, and you give yourself time and grace to build out those different routes, you can begin to change your mindset for *all* future challenges.

9. Letting go

Letting go is hard. It's such a huge topic all by itself, so it would be pointless to tell you it's simple. But I can tell you that if you are able to let go, or hold more lightly, the things that you carry then it will free you. And, once less bound to whatever you were carrying, you will be able to see things differently and have more space to gain breath and perspective about where you are and what you really want.

You may be clinging so hard to old hopes and trying to make them happen, that you haven't stepped back to see whether you still really want these outcomes. Perhaps you are bending yourself out of shape to fit in with a job, a relationship, or expectations of you that don't fit you anymore. You have the option to let them go. Although that sometimes seems impossible and *always* seems scary, it's entirely possible. Nature abhors a vacuum, and the space you make by letting go of the things that don't work will soon be filled with things that more closely align with who you are, and who you hope to become.

So, look down at what you're gripping so tightly on to, and check whether it's still something you really want. If not, prise those fingers of habit off it, and let it go.

10. Watch your words

I can tell you that you're great, and worthy of love and a happy life, because I know that you are. However, me telling you that isn't nearly as powerful as *you* telling *yourself* that, because how you speak to yourself *really* matters. Your self-talk has a direct bearing on outcomes in your life from the granular moment-to-moment all the way up to the bigger picture of your future, because what you *say* often becomes a self-fulfilling prophecy and has a direct bearing on what you do and how you show up in the world. From the simplicity of dropping something and muttering to yourself that you're 'a bloody idiot', to telling yourself that you got made redundant because you're useless at your job, or that you got a poor mark on your exam because you're stupid — they all count, and unfortunately your brain will believe you because it *is* you.

Idiot, boring, stupid, unlovable, weak or useless are some of the many sticks we can all beat ourselves up with. One of these little moments of self-loathing chat might not seem important or impactful, but they all add to the sum total of our internal dialogue, which is one of the only conversations we can't turn and walk away from. How can you expect to feel hopeful when you're telling yourself how rubbish you are? In a world that provides no end of harsh words if you go looking for them (and even when you don't), why don't you choose to be the reliable source of kind words for yourself. Instead of 'a failure' why don't you tell yourself you're brave to have tried, and you're great at learning? Instead of 'weak', why not tell yourself that you're building strength, you're empathic, in touch with your emotions or just taking time to rest? And instead of 'unlovable', well, that is never, ever true. You are eminently, inherently lovable, so park that phrase for good. We don't have to berate ourselves. We get no prizes for self-deprecation and crushing our own confidence; it doesn't improve anything except your level of hopelessness, and we're not moving in that direction. Captain of your own team, remember? And the whole darned cheerleading squad too.

Be generous with your journey

Lastly, remember that captains *lead*. They set an example and they share their failings in order to raise the team up. Don't deny your defeats and hide from your own truths. You know where you've screwed up.

You know when you've made a decision based on values you don't really believe in, like greed, shame or ego. Look right in the face of these uncomfortable feelings — they are the poles of your true North. The discomfort you're feeling is your true nature trying to pull the compass needle back in line. Back ... aligned.

Once you know where you messed up, be generous with it. Shine a light, for the people who are coming up beside and behind you. Shout out, offer a hand, raise your friends, family and colleagues up over the obstacles and explain how you knew they were there. If they don't listen and they trip, just help them up and keep leading, with one light always shining backwards for people to follow you, and one shining forward — the Hope Flame — taking you to where you need to be.

Nothing is quite as fulfilling as being able to help others, especially to help them from the mistakes you yourself have made. Nothing is for nothing — there is always gold to find.

Sometimes when things feel adrift or hopeless, you forget that there is still goodness to be found exactly where you are. Nothing is all bad. But sometimes you need to dig a little deeper and wait. Once you can see and appreciate the good there already is, you can use that to not only see first-hand your ability to cultivate some light in the darkness, but also to have a deeper appreciation of the life you have, so you can springboard from it to the life you want.

10

A little bit of hope goes a long way

Most of the important things in the world have been accomplished by people who have kept on trying when there seemed to be no hope at all.

Dale Carnegie

Sometimes, no matter what wisdom and support is offered, it feels that hope is lost. You may have reached the end of this book with no lift in spirits, no feeling of a light shining at the end of the tunnel. You may have absorbed these words lightly, deflecting them from your inside pain with cynicism or just by feeling too busy to engage. You may think it doesn't apply to you because …

— There have been just too many problems.

— It's too much to solve.

— No one understands.

— You have passed any sense of equilibrium. You are lost.

— There is no longer any way you can see yourself of use, or as a capable and worthy person who deserves to feel hopeful.

— Your job is lost.

— You have fallen behind on your studies.

— You are failing your exams.

— Your relationships are tanking.

- You don't know where you will find the money.

- You have sunk and have no energy to explain.

- You don't fit in or have any desire to try.

- You know that somehow you have become more self-centred than ever. It's only to survive, but you hate it about yourself.

- You don't have any sense of purpose.

- Hope, resilience and perseverance are childish and idealistic concepts — what is the point of having these when you think you are already too far gone? You can't see a way out.

This might be you; it might have been you before now, or it might be you one day.

Lost. Adrift. But hear me out for one final tale. A little story that proves your power to be a purposeful vessel for hope, even when you yourself may feel hopeless.

You may never know the difference you make

At my lowest ebb, I was still teaching. I could muster no purpose for myself; had lost close friendships, my romantic relationship, and trust in my body. I'd withdrawn from almost every gathering, sports race, event, birthday party and social situation in my life. I was lying to my family and friends about how much pain I was in, and I could feel myself shrinking like the pinpoint of light you'd see on an old television set when the power was switched off. All energy had ceased to flow, and all that remained was the tiny spark of light left in the system before total darkness. I chose to use this light for my students.

I had taught for years. It was, and remains, my passion to help shine people's light back to them, to help them see all their potential, purpose and power by just giving them a space to feel seen, heard and safe. I may have been a teacher of English, history and philosophy, but really, I'd always understood the delivery of those subjects as a pleasurable side quest to the real work; the work of getting students to believe in themselves. My role as a successful educator has long been that of a bridge from potential to self-belief. I've stood across the gap for hundreds of people, to show that there is a path for them to their greatest selves. I am to be walked through, or jumped off. It's such a privilege and affords the most incredible viewpoint.

I didn't know all of this back then. I just knew that I had to keep going to work. I had to keep getting into my car in agony, the pain never really receding long enough for me to catch my breath. I took the painkillers, lugged the huge bags of books I'd marked, and moved through the hustling corridors of the secondary school towards my classroom. And there, towards the end of one academic year, I gave out cards to my students as usual.

This year was a little different though, as this year I was considering ending my own life as I celebrated theirs. I used my spark of light for them, and that felt good. They didn't know how I felt, but from my lowest ebb I looked outside of myself, and that kept me going another day, and another, and another.

Fifteen years on, that day in the classroom suddenly came back into my life when I needed it the most.

I was going through another tough time. Unrelated to my chronic pain, thankfully, which, for once, I was managing. I was heartbroken, having moved out of my partner's house after our relationship ended. It didn't help that his house was next door to mine. We had fallen in love through early lockdown, talking through the garden fence and keeping each other's spirits up. I'd fallen equally in love with his three wonderful children. And now, back behind my own walls, I heard them and saw them all, every day, but had lost my role in their lives that I'd held for the past two years. I'd also just been diagnosed with ADHD and was in a deep void of communication and support between the diagnosis and the medical prescribing team. Almost five months of silence and not knowing what to do with my symptoms and the grief I was experiencing as I tried to view the world, myself and my past through a new lens of neurodiversity. All in all, a terrible storm of sadness, loss and confusion, and I felt like I was losing my grip, and losing my hold on hope.

As I've done in the past, I put my thoughts on my social media, sharing that I was suffering and was trying to push through. I try to be honest when I share with my community, but even full honesty eluded me, steeped as I was with the shame of my failed relationship, adrift on the new-diagnosis cross tides of who I really was, versus who I thought I *had* been all my life.

So, I posted on Instagram about the beautiful light through clouds I had seen from my childhood window at my beloved parent's home, and was honest about my struggle:

The light really made me feel awe.

Also though, I have had two panic-attack sobbing meltdowns this weekend too, so I'm ready to see goodness anywhere it shows up.

ADHD meds are still increasing each week (today gone up to 50mg) PLUS two or three other big life things to deal with, means that the process of titration is made much harder and a little scary. It's not how I would have liked this process to be, but I'm going day by day. There are many good things to be thankful for, and the meds are mostly brilliant. I think maybe just getting used to them increasing makes me wobbly, as they can cause insomnia, jitters and anxiety too. I know it'll be okay. Just trying to be honest about it all — it's not all rosy so we can't pretend it is, but nothing ever stays the same: good or bad. Onwards and much love! <3

This was honest. But not the whole truth. I was at the lowest ebb I could remember for years and didn't have the courage or the words to share it properly. I believed no one could help, and the strangled silent-sob phone calls to my parents and sister left them so deeply worried — they were there and ready to help, but nothing seemed to reach me.

And then.

I received a message in my inbox. A message in reply to my Instagram post from Sara, a student I'd taught all those years before.

'*Hello,*' it began:

I'm not sure if you remember me, but I was one of your A level philosophy and ethics students. I've loved following your journey on here and am in awe of what you have achieved! I'm sorry to hear you're having

*a tough time at the moment and thought I would
message and thank you for a time you helped when I
was having a tough time during my A levels all those
years ago, and offer anything I can do to help <3.*

She then posted a photograph. Underneath was this message:

*I found this a couple of years ago at my dad's house
and thought you might like a reminder of all the
people you've helped and inspired over the years,
and how much it meant to them.*

The photograph was of the inside of a card, filled with
writing. My writing. A card I had written to this student
15 years before when my pain was spiralling out of control,
and I was that dwindling point of light in the centre of
a television before there was only a black screen. I was
winking out into nothingness, yet I'd reached out to lift
another person, and now that light was reaching back out
over time and space to lift me.

My words of hope and encouragement, written for Sara
at my lowest ebb, were now also speaking to me:

Dear Sara,

*It's been an absolute pleasure teaching you and
getting to know you over the past few years. I will
be sad not to see you go through Year 13, but I know
you'll be as impressive as ever.*

*If you remember one thing as you go through Uni
and beyond, then it should be to continue keeping
your self-belief and confidence high. You are an
awesome, bright and beautiful young woman with
an incredible future ahead — and don't you forget it
when times get tough. You've had a hell of a time over*

the last 12 months and your poise, gracefulness and courage have continued to impress me.

You'll be a fantastic doctor, or anything else you choose. In the meantime, though, have a crazy (in a good way!) summer and a well-deserved break.

Take care, Miss Muller.

P.S. I was attempting to get a copy of Kahlil Gibran's The Prophet *to you but couldn't find one. Read it, it's perfect for everything (nearly!)*

This student had valued this card. Enough to save it in a box somewhere. She'd connected with the message, and it hadn't made its way to the recycling or the bin. That little pinprick of light had stayed with her, and when it was time, she had passed it back, and my goodness it made all the difference.

None of us knew it then, but we were going to lose my wonderful dad in that same year, too. But not that day. On that day, I ran to him by the fire in the living room in the house I'd grown up in and I showed him the messages.

'Dad!' I'd sobbed.

'What now?!' His consternation was clear.

'No, Dad. It's good. Read it. It's a beautiful thing.'

My dad wasn't one for displays of emotion. Pragmatic, stoic and deeply loving in his own ways, he would walk over glass in bare feet for us all, but he wouldn't often show his feelings. But once he'd put his glasses on and squinted at the screen of my phone, holding it delicately with his hardworking hands, he looked up with tears filming his eyes.

'There!' he said gruffly. 'There it is.'

He continued: 'This is you, Gail. I don't know why you give yourself such a hard time. This is what you can do, who you are, who we see. If you can't believe in us and yourself right now, then believe in this.' And he pushed the phone back into my hand. 'Please, Gail. Why can't you see it?'

'I do, Dad. I do.' And I meant it. Although the year was still to score us all with seemingly unstaunchable wounds, in this moment I saw what he saw, what my students saw, what my family and friends saw but what I was struggling to see. That my feeling hopeless wasn't an objective reality, it was just how I was feeling at that moment. That there were other moments that could come, that had been before, that would be again. If I wanted my students to believe in themselves, to have hope, courage and resilience, then who was I to not follow the same advice I had given them? If they could weather all those storms, then so could I. There I was, reminded by the me of years past, that I always have the light. You have that same light too, and no matter how tiny that pinprick of light is, it can stay bright and strong as it's passed from you, to others, and then back to you again when you need it most.

Hope, truly, springs eternal.

So, it was in this role of reaching out even when I felt I had nothing to give, that I accidentally saved my future self. It's truly in the service of others that we can find ourselves and our reason to keep going.

If you're feeling hopeless and you've scoured every inch of the dusty tundra inside for answers, then I urge you to look beyond, to see who you can lift with a pinpoint of light. Observe how your efforts to raise the tide for another lifts your boat too, and see those lights get brighter.

**Promise me you'll always remember:
You're braver than you believe,
and stronger than you seem,
and smarter than you think.**

Christopher Robin to his best friend Winnie the Pooh,
Pooh's Grand Adventure

Resources

Books to lift, encourage, challenge and galvanize
Big Magic — Elizabeth Gilbert
Fear and Loathing in Las Vegas — Hunter S. Thompson
Glittering a Turd — Kris Hallenga
The Lord of the Rings — J.R.R. Tolkien
Man's Search for Meaning — Viktor Frankl
The Power of Now — Eckhart Tolle
The Prophet — Kahlil Gibran
Winners — Alastair Campbell

Podcasts to bring hope and encouragement
Glittering a Turd — Kris Hallenga
Happy Place — Fearne Cotton
Oprah's Super Soul
We Can Do Hard Things — Glennon Doyle

Hopeful DO Lectures
thedolectures.com
Giles Duley
Eduardo Garcia
Kris Hallenga
Cheryl Strayed & Libby DeLana
... and Gail Muller

About the author

Gail Muller is a Cornish adventurer, author and speaker with a background in education. She has spent twenty years teaching, leading and consulting in the UK and internationally, helping raise aspirations and encouraging life-long learning in both young people and adults.

She has faced a raft of adversity in her life so far, and has moved through considerable challenges with hope, courage, and the passionate belief that our broken bits are actually *superpowers*. Recently diagnosed with ADHD at 44, she also struggled for fifteen years with muscular-skeletal issues and the resulting chronic pain. In 2019, after considerable physical rehabilitation, she set out to walk the Appalachian Trail in the USA, later writing a bestselling book about the experience called *Unlost*. Happily she has stayed well, exploring many long trails since.

Gail is an advocate for living a life that's courageous and true to oneself. She embraces this wholeheartedly and enjoys adventure, writing, exploring and inspiring others to do the same. She is also a coach, running popular online courses and residential retreats in Cornwall, encouraging people to dig into their creativity, build resilience, and grow in confidence. She enjoys hiking long distances and giving talks and workshops all over the world. She lives, hikes and sea swims in Cornwall.

gailmuller.com | *@thegailmuller*

Thanks, beyond measure...

To my tremendous dad, Nick Muller, who would be gruffly bursting with pride that this book is out in the world. 'You've got books to write' he would say, and he was right. More to come Dad, I promise. I'm going forward with my head up, endlessly proud that I'm your daughter.

To my joyous, smart, and endlessly supportive mama, Linda Muller, who inspires and encourages me daily, writes beautifully, and has always done so.

To my talented, brilliant, hardworking, and inspiring sister, Nicky Muller. She might be younger than me, but I've looked up to her for as long as I can remember being able to look up. Hilarious, so determined, so brave and so bright. I'm forever grateful that she captained my team when I couldn't.

To my cherished nieces, Darcy and Agnes, who are the epitome of joyful, loving, hopeful and resilient curiosity. And to their dad Allan, a wonderful husband to my sister and brilliant brother-in-law to me.

To my Muller family; Uncle Tony, Auntie Ann, Fergus, Rebecca and Aine.

To my Cormack family; Uncle Ian; who has helped make so many good things become possible, Auntie Christine, Sally, Jamie, Jerry and Lee.

To my dear friend Kris Hallenga, who believed in me, and was the catalyst behind me being able to share my words, thoughts, and story. She has enabled me to lift more people up, just as she has been lifting so many for so long.

To wonderful Giovanna Fletcher, who trusted that I could write a story as well as I could tell it around the campfire in the Himalayan mountains one starry October a few years ago. Thanks, my friend, for believing in me, and helping me start on this path.

To Charlotte Ilsley, a remarkable and special young woman who helped me remember my purpose in a dark time.

To my editor and publisher Miranda West, who knew I had a story to share and believed that I could help people by the telling of it. And my wonderful agent Hannah Ferguson, who never stops supporting and encouraging me in my writing journey.

To Cornwall, for its rich wealth of natural and abundant beauty, and to the Cornish people I am proud to be one of, with our communities, traditions, and ways of life on land and sea.

And finally, to Hope: my friend, my ally, and the kindling for the flame that keeps me burning with a desire to do better, give freely, and live fully.

Books in the series

Do Agile Tim Drake

Do Beekeeping Orren Fox

Do Birth Caroline Flint

Do Bitcoin Angelo Morgan-Somers

Do Breathe
Michael Townsend Williams

Do Build Alan Moore

Do Deal
Richard Hoare & Andrew Gummer

Do Death Amanda Blainey

Do Design Alan Moore

Do Disrupt Mark Shayler

Do Drama Lucy Gannon

Do Earth Tamsin Omond

Do Fly Gavin Strange

Do Grow Alice Holden

Do Hope Gail Muller

Do Improvise Robert Poynton

Do Inhabit Sue Fan & Danielle Quigley

Do Interesting Russell Davies

Do Lead Les McKeown

Do Listen Bobette Buster

Do Make James Otter

Do Open David Hieatt

Do Pause Robert Poynton

Do Photo Andrew Paynter

Do Present Mark Shayler

Do Preserve
Anja Dunk, Jen Goss & Mimi Beaven

Do Protect Johnathan Rees

Do Purpose David Hieatt

Do Scale Les McKeown

Do Sea Salt
Alison, David & Jess Lea-Wilson

Do Sing James Sills

Do Sourdough Andrew Whitley

Do Start Dan Kieran

Do Story Bobette Buster

Do Team Charlie Gladstone

Do Walk Libby DeLana

Do Wild Baking Tom Herbert

Also available

The Book of Do A manual for living edited by Miranda West

Path A short story about reciprocity Louisa Thomsen Brits

The Skimming Stone A short story about courage Dominic Wilcox

Stay Curious How we created a world class event in a cowshed Clare Hieatt

The Path of a Doer A simple tale of how to get things done David Hieatt

Available in print, digital and audio formats from booksellers or via our website: **thedobook.co**

To hear about events and forthcoming titles, find us on social media **@dobookco**, or subscribe to our newsletter